PRAISE FOR
POST-ACQUISITION MARKETING

In my twenty-plus years of investing, Shiv is the best marketing strategist I have ever met. This book is a must-read for any private equity investor or CEO wanting to accelerate growth in a B2B technology business.

—BRYCE YOUNGREN, MANAGING
PARTNER AT POLARIS PARTNERS

Every CEO of a PE-backed company should read Post-Acquisition Marketing. Shiv opened my eyes to the power of rethinking marketing alignment and accountability. We followed the roadmap laid out in this book to turn marketing into a force-multiplier for revenue growth. The results are undeniable.

—BILL HAYES, CEO AT TOP OF MIND

I've seen the power of Shiv's framework firsthand inside two PE-backed software companies where moving with speed using a data-driven revenue generation model was critical. Post-Acquisition Marketing is a how-to guide for B2B executives looking to understand the 'why' behind what budget to allocate to marketing.

—KELLY CONNERY, PRESIDENT AT OECONNECTION

Yes! Finally a celebration of smart marketing investments—the moves that help you win deals instead of just raising awareness. This book is a rallying cry to ensure marketers are equipped to embrace big growth targets by looking at the numbers and making smart business decisions.

—MIKE DEVINE, CMO OF HELPSYSTEMS

Post-Acquisition Marketing covers what matters to PE investors: the importance of data in all critical board decisions. Every entrepreneur that wants to build toward an exit and scale with a PE partner needs to follow the process outlined in this book.

—ZANE TARENCE, PARTNER AND MANAGING DIRECTOR AT FOUNDERS ADVISORS

At the intersection of M&A and organic growth is where substantive value is created...or consequently squandered. Post-Acquisition Marketing is a must-read for all who want to maximize value creation for their portfolio investments.

—TONY REISZ, CEO AT WEST LEDGE ADVISORS

Shiv understands how tech investors think. Post-Acquisition Marketing gives investors and CEOs a clear framework to successfully scale demand generation to generate investment returns.

—DEEPAK SINDWANI, MANAGING PARTNER AT WAVECREST GROWTH PARTNERS

As the Founder and CEO of a PE-backed company, I'm all too familiar with the lofty expectations that come with an acquisition. Shiv and the How To SaaS team used the framework outlined in this book to transform our company's go-to-market strategy and turned marketing into a consistent, predictable revenue driver.

—WILL BOUDREAUX, CEO AT NETCHEX

Post-Acquisition Marketing gives the next generation of leaders a clear roadmap for creating inflection points in their businesses by leveraging data-driven marketing and focusing on metrics that matter.

—RONAN KENNEDY, DIRECTOR AT B CAPITAL GROUP

Post-Acquisition Marketing cuts through the common BS by approaching marketing as the precise discipline it is meant to be. Using appropriate KPIs to directly link activities and outcomes to specific business goals, this book helps build the accountability framework for marketing teams to deliver results.

—DMITRY BUTERIN, FOUNDER AND FORMER CEO OF WILD APRICOT

POST-ACQUISITION MARKETING

POST-ACQUISITION M▲RKETING

HOW TO CREATE ENTERPRISE VALUE IN THE FIRST 100 DAYS

Shiv Narayanan

LIONCREST
PUBLISHING

POST-ACQUISITION MARKETING
How to Create Enterprise Value in the First 100 Days

ISBN   978-1-5445-1997-5   *Hardcover*
       978-1-5445-1996-8   *Paperback*
       978-1-5445-1995-1   *Ebook*
       978-1-5445-2045-2   *Audiobook*

Author photograph by Katy Chan

CONTENTS

All the stories in this book are real, from situations we encounter every day with our clients at How To SaaS. Details—company names, people, products, revenue numbers, market intelligence, financials—have been altered and fictionalized to preserve confidentiality and protect sensitive information.

INTRODUCTION

"You can't manage what you don't measure."
—PETER DRUCKER

"I need to know the truth, and I need to know it fast."

Those were Henry's first words on his first call with me, shortly after Fleetsync, his fleet-management software company, was acquired by the private equity firm North Star Capital.

Henry was the new CEO, who had taken over as the two founders transitioned out after the acquisition. He got the role because, in his former position as COO, he had helped build the business to this point. The board trusted him to lead the company through the transition.

"We've got really ambitious targets to hit next year. I'm going to need to scale Marketing to get there," he said. "But I'm not going to invest any more of our budget until I understand the data behind it."

Henry was understandably frustrated because he was flying blind. His VP of Marketing insisted they were adding tons of value to the company, but his new VP of Sales disagreed. He had no way to judge who was right. Even worse, he had no time to figure it out.

As COO, Henry had helped build a $30 million business that was profitable and already growing fast—which is what led to the buyout in the first place. But post-acquisition, he had to face aggressive sales projections, shortened timelines, and a hyper-focus on efficiency and financial discipline.

It was unfamiliar territory.

What Henry didn't realize was that he wasn't the only one who found himself in this position. Every year, fast-growing, profitable companies emerge. Every year, private equity acquires those companies and sets aggressive expectations for growth. And every year, those companies run into the same problem: they need more pipeline to hit their sales targets but don't know how to scale Marketing to get there.

With ambitious expectations, scaling Marketing becomes a pivotal growth lever. The problem is that most marketing organizations do not have their data in order. Without data, it is impossible to illustrate the ROI of marketing activities. If you can't illustrate the ROI of marketing activities, it is impossible to get approval for increased budget. And if you can't get increased budget, it is impossible to scale Marketing.

This problem is not about size either. A company doing $10 million in ARR needs to get its data in order just as much as one doing $300 million. In fact, as companies get bigger, the complexity increases. There are more acquisitions to integrate, more opportunities to capture, and more data to manage.

Very few marketing organizations can tell you their impact on revenue back to exact dollars invested in specific programs, campaigns, and channels. They may be able to tell you their contribution to pipeline, but there is a lot of fuzziness around what "contribution" actually means.

Post-acquisition, there can be no room for fuzziness.

Private equity investors buy companies like Henry's after intense, data-driven due diligence cycles—financial, legal, sales, technical, market, customer—to triangulate the true potential of a particular business. The ultimate objective is to create enterprise value and increase the overall valuation of the business.

The stakes are high. Jobs are on the line. Hundreds of millions of dollars hang in the balance.

Unfortunately, Marketing teams are underprepared to play their role because most organizations do not look to Marketing as a primary generator of revenue, and therefore don't give it the right amount of budget to succeed.

SHIFTING MARKETING'S ACCOUNTABILITY

I sat down with Henry to understand his frustrations more. He had fired two VPs of Sales in the last three years. Kyle, his current VP of Sales, was the third person to hold the role in as many years.

"Neither of the last two VPs were delivering," said Henry. "The majority of our sales reps were missing quota, and I just couldn't allow that to continue."

"Why will this time be different?" I asked.

"It may not be," Henry shot back. "Kyle needs to prove he can play at this level."

Sales leaders with short tenures are not all that uncommon. According to Salesforce's *State of Sales* report, the average tenure of a VP of Sales has declined from 26 months in 2010 to 18 months in 2020. VPs of Sales are hired, given 18 months to prove themselves, and then replaced if they don't deliver. This turnover is expensive, costing hundreds of thousands of dollars in hiring, firing, and onboarding costs.

While CEOs, executives, and investors could potentially be more patient in some of these instances, they often don't have a choice. They have ambitious targets to hit, and they have to hold everyone accountable when the numbers don't add up.

The biggest contributing factor to VPs of Sales getting fired is, as in Henry's company, when their sales reps miss quota. According to the same State of Sales report, 57% of reps miss quota.

When I shared this data point with Henry, he pulled up a sales dashboard of all the Fleetsync sales reps. 54% of them had missed quota last year. Henry couldn't believe it. How did his company have roughly the same number of ineffective salespeople as the market? Did he fire two VPs of Sales prematurely? Was Kyle headed toward a similar fate?

It was certainly possible, but I needed to understand more about the Go-To-Market organization inside Henry's company before I could diagnose the root cause.

"Tell me more about the Marketing function," I said, turning the conversation's focus. "Why do you think there is a problem?"

"Kyle is constantly complaining about the quality of leads," Henry explained. "But Nicole, my VP of Marketing, claims she's generating a lot of awareness for us in the market."

This was the root cause of the he-said-she-said debate between Sales and Marketing inside Henry's company. His Sales team was continuing to miss quota, while Marketing was washing its hands clean after leads were handed off to reps. Growth targets were at risk, and no one really knew what was going wrong.

From Nicole's perspective, she was doing everything she could. The Marketing team was primarily focused on events, sales enablement, and product marketing. Nicole had a small team of 7 people: a product marketer, a sales enablement manager, an event specialist, a content writer, a web developer, an email marketer, and a designer. Nicole was herself involved in the day-to-day execution of marketing tasks to fill in the gaps of the marketing function.

The team drove pipeline from six key trade shows a year, created content to support the sales and product teams, ran email marketing campaigns and monthly webinars, and invested a modest amount in paid media. Their total marketing budget for the year was $1.2 million for both headcount and programs for a company that was doing $30 million in revenue with 4 product lines.

For a company with aspirations of growing 30% year over year organically, allocating only 4% of revenue toward Marketing is a recipe for disaster. It meant almost the entire responsibility of growth rested on the shoulders of Sales.

No wonder sales reps were missing quota. They had the gargantuan task of sourcing, nurturing, and closing enough pipeline to grow the business by 30% every year. And they were doing it alone.

"This is solvable," I reassured Henry. "We're going to get this train on the tracks really fast, but it is going to take a commitment from you to guide the organization through a transformation."

"What kind of transformation?" asked Henry.

"The kind where Marketing is accountable to revenue," I explained.

Nicole's $1.2 million Marketing budget did not have any revenue targets associated with it. Instead, Marketing was treated like a cost center at Fleetsync. It was given budget not to increase revenue but to support Sales in whatever it needed.

There was a good reason for this. Fleetsync, like many companies, began as a Sales-led organization. The two founders came from the logistics space and had many relationships that they sold into to get the company off the ground. As the company grew, they slowly hired people to replace themselves in each of their sales roles to move away from a founder-led sales model.

Over time, the culture and strategy to grow Fleetsync was simple: Sales was responsible for revenue growth. Product served Sales. Client Services served Sales. And Marketing served Sales.

Marketing's role became narrowly focused on one objective: help Sales close more deals. As a result, marketing activities focused on the items that will deliver the most value to the sales team such as sales enablement, events, and product marketing. Marketing was not responsible for bookings. It was merely a participant, a supporting cast member.

Shockingly, this is the reality of Marketing inside many B2B companies. They have limited budgets and small teams because they are only expected to support ambitious sales targets. I've seen numerous companies doing north of $100 million in revenue with a marketing team of less than 10 people.

It may seem like a head-scratcher, but it's not. These companies are relics of the old world, where Sales was the only rainmaker.

In this hierarchy, Nicole and the Marketing team could hide behind catchphrases like "We are building the brand" or "We're providing air cover for our Sales team." It also made it more difficult for Henry to hold Marketing accountable. Did scanning 500 badges at that conference really help the company? Was it worth spending $25,000 on that booth? Was this more or less effective than simply taking the list of attendees and sending them an email?

Nicole's Marketing team never had good answers for these

questions because they were never expected to focus on the data that showcased their ROI. It was never part of their accountability.

This problem becomes magnified in a private equity environment after an acquisition. Private equity investors expect Marketing to take on greater responsibility for revenue and bring data to guide decisions to help the company reach its expectations. Unfortunately, most marketing organizations don't have any of this data in place to meet those expectations.

In other words, data is private equity's native language, and Marketing needs to speak it. Without data, Marketing will continue to be relegated to second-class status indefinitely—a supporting cast member when it needs it to be a star.

This is why Henry needed to know the truth. He needed to get Marketing performing at an elite level for the company to have any shot at delivering on North Star Capital's investment thesis.

MARKETING IN THE FIRST 100 DAYS

I worked with Nicole to dig more deeply into Fleetsync's marketing data. I wanted to know the difference in close rates depending on the source of deals in the pipeline. It turned out that Marketing Generated Pipeline had a close rate of over 43%, while Sales Generated Pipeline had a close rate of only 23%.

Despite this glaring statistic, Fleetsync's Marketing budget was, again, only 4% of revenue, while Sales had 20%. Wouldn't a company focused on growth give Marketing more budget so that more deals would close?

They would have to be crazy not to.

Why, then, did Nicole not have more budget for Marketing? The short answer is that even VPs of Marketing, like Nicole, haven't figured out all the ways in which Marketing can drive enterprise value and how to lobby for more budget. When I asked Nicole to pull that report, the data was all there and within reach. She had just never looked at it or shared it with Henry.

How could Henry or the board ever give more budget to Marketing if they weren't educated on its value and ROI?

The role of Marketing inside companies that is often neglected and underestimated is quantifying and communicating its value internally and upward. This work is especially important in the first 100 days after an acquisition.

Leading up to the acquisition, private equity investors build an investment thesis to deliver on once the transaction is completed. This investment thesis identifies the biggest value-creation levers inside a business. Items that are commonly found in the investment thesis and are considered core strategic growth levers include scaling new bookings, acquiring and integrating additional companies, capturing white space opportunity, increasing prices, introducing additional products or supply chain steps, and entering new markets.

While Marketing has a vital role to play in delivering on all aspects of the investment thesis, each of the above levers could be a book in and of itself. For our purposes, we will focus on scaling new bookings, as it is inevitably part of every investment thesis. It is also the area where Marketing has the biggest room to make an impact as a primary role-player to create enterprise value.

In Henry's case, he needed to show North Star Capital that his Marketing and Sales engine was set up for success by his first board meeting, which was scheduled for (coincidentally) exactly 100 days after the acquisition. The board wanted to see quick wins to validate their investment thesis and feel confident in the Marketing strategy for the next year to ensure that sales projections would be met.

This is why North Star Capital introduced me to Henry and brought me into Fleetsync as soon as the transaction closed.

It was the same call I've received from countless investors and CEOs. Each has a company with ambitious targets, and each needs to scale Marketing to get there.

Over the next 3 months, I worked closely with Nicole to get Fleetsync's marketing data in order, stopped investing in unprofitable channels, scaled programs with positive ROI, launched new demand generation campaigns, and identified key gaps in the team. With this work, Henry was able to get the transparency into Marketing's impact that he was looking for, and we were able to increase Fleetsync's marketing budget by 50% after presenting data-backed business cases to the board.

All within the first 100 days after the acquisition.

The results? In the following 12 months, Fleetsync saw a 300% increase in Marketing Generated Pipeline and Closed Won deals.

This kind of result is not an anomaly. In almost every market, companies are heavily underleveraged and under-indexed in marketing and demand generation.

In the upcoming chapters, I'm going to walk you through my 5-step framework to scale Marketing to create more enterprise value in the first 100 days after an acquisition. It's the same framework I took Henry and Fleetsync through. It's the same framework I've deployed as the CEO of How To SaaS with hundreds of other companies in different markets, verticals, and industries. I've even used it myself as the CMO of Wild Apricot, which was eventually acquired by Rubicon Technology Partners in 2017 and flipped to Pamlico Capital in 2018.

It works. It will work for you too.

By the end of this book, you'll have an exact plan to turn your marketing function into a data-driven revenue generator that can create enterprise value for your business. You'll have more budget for Marketing than ever before.

And you'll know precisely how to use it to scale faster.

MARKETING DUE DILIGENCE

"Accountability breeds response-ability."
—STEPHEN COVEY

"We spent $1 million on LinkedIn Ads in the last 12 months alone," said Cameron. "I want to figure out how to double that spend in the next 6 months."

It was June 2020. We were a few months into the first round of COVID lockdowns. Cameron was the CEO of Pass Spring, a password management solution for enterprises. The company had already crossed $50 million in revenue in 2020 after an astronomical Q2 for bookings. IT teams building the security infrastructure to enable their remote workers were implementing the solution at record speed.

Spartan Technology Partners, Pass Spring's private equity sponsor, had encouraged Cameron to bring me on to help figure out how to scale the company's Marketing faster.

Cameron was as motivated a CEO as I had met. He knew the market had presented his company with a golden opportunity to scale Pass Spring faster. His killer instinct was to ensure the company was doing everything it could, from a marketing standpoint, to scale.

"$1 million is impressive," I said to Cameron and his Director of Marketing, Patricia. "Most B2B companies struggle to scale LinkedIn Ads to that point."

"Thanks," said Patricia, gleaming with pride. "We know

IT professionals are on LinkedIn, so we've been targeting them based on their job title since last year."

"And how has that been performing?" I asked.

"Really well," said Patricia. "We're generating about 50 leads a week from LinkedIn alone."

"How do you define a lead?" I asked.

"Anyone who has filled out a form for a white paper or webinar," replied Patricia.

"How many of those leads become Demos or MQLs?"

"Out of the 50 leads being generated monthly from LinkedIn, about 10 get to MQL status."

"That's fantastic," I said. "So about 20% of your leads are becoming MQLs."

"Yes, that sounds about right."

"What percentage of those MQLs become Closed Won deals?" I asked.

"We don't know," Patricia answered. "We report out till

MQL in HubSpot. When the lead enters Salesforce, the sales team tracks that."

That's when Cameron jumped back in, "That data is in Salesforce, isn't it, Patricia?"

"I really don't know," she responded. "I'm never really in there."

Cameron started sharing his screen. He pulled up a Salesforce reporting dashboard for lead source. After tinkering with it for a few minutes, he found the report that gave the answer I was looking for.

There was a pause as the report highlighted the results of the campaign. The $1 million in LinkedIn ads had produced 537 leads, 129 demos, 7 opportunities, and only 2 closed won deals.

Spend	$1,000,000
Leads	537
Demos	129
Opportunities	7
Cost/Opportunity	$143,000
Closed Won	2
Average Deal Size	$25,000
CAC	$500,000

This meant that Pass Spring had spent $500,000 in Customer Acquisition Costs and $143,000 per opportunity. Their average deal size per customer was only $25,000.

$950,000 in ad spend wasted. Unbelievable.

"Does this sound right to you, Patricia?" Cameron asked in disbelief.

Patricia didn't have an answer. She had never connected her work on the Marketing side through to revenue.

UNDERSTANDING COSTLY MISTAKES

For a company like Pass Spring, growing as fast as they were, flaws in Marketing are easily covered up. There are so many leads, demos, and opportunities that poor data and revenue accountability go unnoticed. This is a dangerous position to be in because when something breaks, you have no idea of how you should fix it.

And things do break. All the time.

Scaling Marketing faster is always the goal, but doing so without the right data and accountability framework in place often means burning through valuable capital. It is not like flipping a switch. It's about building an engine that is predictable so that more dollars can be invested with confidence as time goes on.

After the meeting, Cameron asked to chat with me 1-on-1. "I'm a little embarrassed," he said. "We started that conversation by telling you how much we're spending on LinkedIn as a sign of success, and it turns out we don't know what we're doing."

"Building a $50 million company is nothing to be embarrassed about," I said. "With how fast you're growing, something was going to be missed somewhere."

"Yes, but isn't this why we have Patricia?" he asked. "How could Patricia let a mistake like this happen?"

"Well," I responded, "how many times have you looked at that Salesforce dashboard yourself? Is Patricia accountable to you and the company for demos booked or for closed won deals?"

"Unfortunately, I've only held her accountable to an MQL target," replied Cameron sheepishly. "I talk to my VP of Sales about opportunities and overall deals closed."

This answer was at the root of the problem. Marketing's accountability at Pass Spring stopped at the MQLs generated, while Sales was held accountable for those leads closing. (Notice, by the way, the striking similarity between this reality and the one faced by Henry inside Fleetsync.)

Within this operational structure, Marketing never has to measure which activity produces the most revenue. Because all MQLs are treated equally, the end goal is to just fill the top of the funnel and report on that to the company. After all, more MQLs mean you're doing a good job, right?

Wrong.

Every marketing activity produces a different kind of lead. Someone who downloads a white paper from a paid social ad is completely different from someone who attended a webinar. Marketing teams deploy lead-scoring metrics to equate some of these activities together. For example, if someone downloaded a white paper and then read 3 blog posts, they are converted to an MQL and treated as equal to someone who signed up for a product demo. But these leads are anything but the same quality.

This is how bad MQLs enter the pipeline. Sales ends up complaining about lead quality, and MQL to Closed Won rates drop. Sales is pressured for not meeting quota. They're enabled with better call scripts, objection-handling responses, and competitive intelligence tools while being told they need to dial for dollars better. Meanwhile, Marketing takes curtain calls at the weekly all-hands meeting about hitting an all-time high in MQLs generated. This is why Sales teams end up hating Marketing in some organizations.

In trying to keep up with their growth, Cameron and Patricia kept investing marketing dollars into channels driving more leads. Any channel that showed a signal got more budget as the company scaled. If leads were coming in, regardless of quality, Patricia kept spending, and Cameron never asked why.

There was never a reason to stop and ask what was working and what wasn't because the company was growing so rapidly.

In essence, Pass Spring was growing despite knowing its marketing data. Without data, they were pursuing expensive initiatives in the dark. They didn't know where to invest or how to track success on those investments. They were playing pin the tail on the donkey. Maybe they guessed right and invested in the right places a few times. That led to the mistaken confidence that anything would work if given enough budget. That's how a $950,000 blunder was made.

"This isn't Patricia's fault or yours," I reassured him. "Pass Spring is growing significantly faster than you can build the right infrastructure and processes to support the growth. This is the work that needs to be done now to help you scale to the next level."

ESTABLISHING THE RIGHT ACCOUNTABILITY METRICS

Over the next few weeks, I worked with Patricia to overhaul what Marketing reported on. The main adjustment we made was establishing two new core metrics to judge Marketing success: Marketing-Generated Pipeline and Closed Won Deals.

By tracking beyond MQLs, we removed Marketing's bias for lead volume and replaced it with lead quality. If Pass Spring's Sales team had a qualification call with a prospect, and they deemed the lead to be a bad fit for any reason, then that lead was removed from the pipeline generated by Marketing. Simple.

This allowed everyone to focus on high-quality prospects and deals that were actually ready to enter the next stage of the funnel. It also removed channel bias. Given that some channels were generating leads who were more ready to buy than others, Marketing-Generated Pipeline told us how many of those leads were actually accepted by Sales. At the MQL level, this is impossible to accomplish with just lead-scoring mechanisms. Now that a sales rep had to call a prospect to verify lead quality, there was new clarity in which channels brought in the best leads.

Once Marketing's accountability was connected to pipeline and revenue, they stopped reporting on vanity metrics like lead volume and began focusing on sales. Every time Sales accepted the lead, they were signaling that the lead quality was good and it could no longer be used as a reason for missing quota.

Most importantly, this change removed excuses on both sides and completely upended the legacy dynamics inside Pass Spring. Instead, the company began ushering in a new era of alignment and teamwork between Marketing and Sales.

"We're spending a lot of time on pulling all this data together," said Patricia. "It's taking time away from actually doing marketing work."

What Patricia felt is how a lot of marketers feel about data and operations work. There is just so much to work on with so few resources that slowing down seems like a major distraction.

"All of this is marketing work," I said. "We're front-loading data work to build the infrastructure for measuring Marketing's impact on the business."

To Patricia, the data work didn't feel like a core marketing activity. It was more of an administrative task that was a pain to pull together. What she missed was that this infrastructure work would help us understand our Acceptable Cost per Lead. Once we knew that, we'd finally have clarity on one of Marketing's key questions: what should be scaled and by how much?

Your acceptable cost per lead is the amount you can spend on each lead and remain profitable, based on how likely that lead is to close. With an Acceptable Cost per Lead figure in place, you can set a baseline to evaluate the success of any marketing activities and avoid burning cash on dead ends.

When Marketing's accountability is tied to MQLs, the way you measure your Acceptable Cost per Lead is by looking at CPA (Cost Per Activation). The CPA implies your cost for any type of lead. Because not all MQLs are created equal, this is a recipe for disaster.

In Patricia's case, her CPA target for her $1 million in LinkedIn ad spend was $2,500. There was a good reason for this. Overall, Pass Spring's funnel conversion rates were high. With their average deal size of $25,000, they were actually closing 10% of MQLs.

By trying to achieve a 12-month payback period, this meant Patricia could spend $2,500 per lead. So when the 537 leads generated from the spend on LinkedIn came in at $1,862 per lead, there was no issue. Patricia was well within her limits to continue spending. It's also why Cameron never hesitated to give Patricia more budget as the leads came in.

However, when we started to look at the pipeline and revenue data, the perception of the numbers changed. 129 of the 537 leads became demos, which is a 24% conversion rate. Of those 129 demos, only 7 became opportunities. That's a 5.4% conversion rate from Demo to Opportunity. Finally, 2 deals out of those 7 opportunities implies a 28.5% Opportunity to Closed Won rate.

Assuming these numbers held, Patricia's Acceptable Cost per Lead for the channel was significantly lower than $2,500. Patricia would need 3.5 opportunities to close 1 deal worth $25,000 at a 28.5% close rate. To generate 3.5 opportunities, Patricia would need 64 demos. To generate 64 demos, Patricia would need 270 leads. Assuming Pass

Spring's average deal size of $25,000, this means that Pass Spring could spend $390 per demo and only $92 per lead.

Deals	1
Opportunities Needed	3.5
Demos Needed	64
Acceptable Cost per Demo	$390
Leads Needed	270
Acceptable Cost per Lead	$92

Needless to say, this was vastly lower than Patricia's actual performance of $1,862 per lead, where all leads were being treated equally.

As we got to these numbers, Patricia was flabbergasted. "I spent 20 times my Acceptable Cost per Lead on LinkedIn?!"

I nodded. "That's why we do this work."

"With this kind of data accountability, I feel more pressure on Marketing to help the organization deliver," said Patricia.

"It's the good kind of pressure," I said. "More pressure means Marketing will get more support, resources, and budget to make more impact."

Reorienting the Marketing organization around pipeline

and revenue also gave Patricia targets to hit for the organization with her marketing budget. Every week, her job was to show how Marketing was tracking against her Marketing Generated Pipeline targets.

She and her Marketing team were accountable for the company's growth just as much as Sales was.

SCALING THE RIGHT CHANNELS AND CAMPAIGNS

Measuring the effectiveness of the LinkedIn campaign was just the first step with Patricia.

"The bigger question is this," I said to Patricia. "Where else could Pass Spring have invested that money?

"It's one thing to find leads that are not profitable," I continued. "But what if there's another channel where that money would have generated a significantly higher return? Wouldn't you want to start allocating more money to that channel or campaign now?"

At the micro level of a campaign, stopping the LinkedIn ads campaign made a lot of sense. The follow-up question, however, was where should Patricia have invested that money instead? After all, there were still growth targets to hit and a marketing budget that needed to be reallocated to get there.

Before we could move that $1 million investment, though, we needed a clear picture of how the entire budget was performing.

Patricia's overall marketing budget was $3.7 million. She was investing about $1.5 million into paid media, of which $1 million went into LinkedIn and the rest was split between Google and Facebook. Another $780,000 was going into trade shows, with an additional $300,000 going into content. The rest was going into Patricia's team salaries and headcount.

Patricia and I went through the same exercise for each channel and campaign that her team had run. This included every ad campaign and every trade show her team invested into.

The trade show channel was quite effective. The $780,000 in spend had generated $1.2 million in revenue for the business in the previous year. The channel was working and generating significant revenue.

As we connected the marketing spend data through to Closed Won, though, it turned out that the 3 biggest health-care trade shows, with a total annual cost of $125,000, generated $974,000 of the $1.2 million pipeline. That was roughly 80% of the revenue from 15% of the spend. Patricia and her team were investing $660,000 every year to generate $226,000 in additional revenue from trade shows, which is $0.34 in ROI for every $1 in marketing spend.

Not only that, but Patricia's team was spending months planning for each show, flying team members down for each show, and investing time in follow-up on the leads they generated. Hundreds of thousands of dollars and months of effort to close deals at an abysmal ROI.

With COVID-19 restricting travel and events altogether, the decision for this channel was easy. All the events were going virtual for the remainder of 2020. Patricia opted out of all of them except one, which was the event that brought in most of the pipeline.

The exercise also opened up an interesting question for Patricia's LinkedIn investments. Was the entire spend useless or just some of it? It turned out that Patricia had 5 campaigns set up on LinkedIn, of which 80% of the demos and the 2 closed won deals came from 1 campaign where only $90,000 had been spent. The rest of the $910,000 in spend went into campaigns that produced a lot of leads but no revenue.

This is a common theme in most channels. True to the Pareto Principle, 80% of the revenue from a channel often comes from 20% of the campaigns. The problem is that companies don't know which 20% is the most effective.

Continuing with the LinkedIn campaign that brought in the revenue made a lot of sense. The Payback Period was more than a year, but that was acceptable. There was enough pipeline to justify optimizing and experimenting with the campaigns.

Between the trade shows and the LinkedIn ads, Patricia's team suddenly had a lot more time and budget to work with. She had freed up over $1.1 million of marketing budget freed up to reallocate.

Meanwhile, Pass Spring was investing about $300,000 a year into Google Ads and an additional $100,000 a year on Facebook, through which they had generated $700,000 and $300,000, respectively, in closed won deals. Between those 2 channels, Pass Spring was generating a 2.5 times Return on Ad Spend on a 5-month Payback Period.

This was another layer to why Cameron and Patricia didn't notice the inefficiency on LinkedIn. There was so much deal volume coming from paid media overall that no one ever looked under the hood to figure out the specifics.

	LinkedIn	Trade Shows	Google Ads	Facebook Ads
Spend	$1,000,000	$780,000	$300,000	$100,000
Revenue	$50,000	$1,200,000	$700,000	$300,000
ROI	5%	153%	233%	300%
Payback Period	20 years	8 months	5 months	4 months

"Those are astronomical numbers for paid media," I said to Patricia. "B2B companies usually struggle to break even on their ad spend in 12 months."

I could tell from Patricia's look that she was thinking the same thing I was.

What if she had taken the wasted LinkedIn spend and allocated additional budget to Google or Facebook? How much farther along would she be now?

CREATING THE RIGHT DEMAND GENERATION STRATEGY

As we analyzed the potential to invest into Google and Facebook for Pass Spring, we found that the potential to scale spend on those channels was north of $3 million per year.

When we presented those numbers to Cameron, he was thrilled. He had wanted to double LinkedIn spend when we first started working together. Now, he had a far more targeted way to scale across his channels.

Building the right accountability framework for Marketing helped Patricia tell Cameron the story of why the focus needed to shift. Cameron was an easy sell. He wasn't attached to any channel. He just wanted to scale Pass Spring faster.

Part of the benefit of going through the exercise is that some of the money was sitting right under Patricia's nose. We used the reallocated $1.1 million of marketing budget available and bet heavily on scaling the Google, Facebook, and LinkedIn campaigns that were working. We also introduced additional channels and campaigns to experiment with to find more places to effectively generate marketing pipeline.

At a board meeting 6 months later, Patricia presented a 200% increase in Marketing Generated Pipeline in the second half of 2020. Pass Spring had done this under her leadership while keeping the marketing budget in check in the most tumultuous year for businesses.

Cameron called me, full of excitement, as soon as the meeting ended. "The board just approved our marketing budget proposal for the full $3 million in 2021."

"Great!" I exclaimed. "But don't get too comfortable. There's still a lot of work ahead."

Data had gotten Cameron and Patricia into a place where their campaigns were all profitable, but to really maximize the value of their marketing dollars, we'd have to keep digging into the data to get that demand gen engine not just up and running but operating at full speed.

DEMAND GENERATION

"The essence of strategy is choosing what not to do."

—MICHAEL PORTER

"It's been a struggle, to be honest," admitted Janice. "Trade shows are the only place we've made any real impact on revenue. That's why I'm not sold on Marketing being able to help us scale."

I nodded in acknowledgment. What Janice didn't know was that I'd heard hundreds of CEOs say the same thing to me before. What she felt is how a lot of CEOs feel before they can figure out how to make Marketing a revenue driver.

Janice was the Founder and CEO of Case Rocket, a case management solution for law firms. At the time, the company was doing about $7 million in revenue—on the smaller end of companies we work with.

Oceanbridge Capital, a growth equity firm focused on mid-market companies, was the first institutional investor Case Rocket had ever had. Janice had bootstrapped the business without any investors over the previous 12 years, which was a major accomplishment. She had done it slowly, cautiously making investments to build the company.

Then Oceanbridge came along and saw a company in a growing market with the potential to scale a lot faster and take market share. They wanted to be aggressive with growth. That's why they invested.

So when I had my first call with Janice, there was no Director or VP of Marketing in place. There was Janice, playing the role of interim CMO—along with being the CEO—and 2 junior marketing coordinators.

Janice had poured her blood, sweat, and tears into Case Rocket. She wanted to grow it faster, but she was having trouble figuring out how.

What's more, massive companies like Clio had been built in the legal tech market, proving Case Rocket could do far better. Janice's sales team came up against Clio on a lot of deals, and Case Rocket won a lot of those showdowns. A lot of customers leaving Clio also found Case Rocket to be a better option. Yet Case Rocket was only a fraction of Clio's size.

Janice felt like she had a great product but an inferior Go-To-Market.

As we ran through the Marketing Due Diligence process, there wasn't much to analyze. Case Rocket was investing less than $300,000 a year on marketing, most of which was going to those trade shows and the salaries of the two junior team members.

When I asked Janice what they had tried on the marketing side beyond the trade shows, the list wasn't very long. They had a team member writing weekly blog posts, and they had run a one-off webinar. They had overhauled their website with an agency, and they had invested a modest amount into ads on Google.

Because she had bootstrapped the company herself, Janice never had C-level marketing expertise on her team to help her figure out how to take the next steps in scaling Marketing. It was always too expensive, and she ended up putting any available capital toward Sales and Product, like many founders do.

"This is an opportunity," I said to Janice. "You don't have to behave like a startup anymore because you have institutional capital behind you. That means we can try things you have never tried before. When you were bootstrapping the business, you had to squeeze every dollar to make sure you didn't overextend yourself. Now we can invest more aggressively if we can showcase the right thinking to the board."

UNDERSTANDING THE BUSINESS CONTEXT

What Janice and Case Rocket had done on the marketing side is what most companies do. They started by attending trade shows where their market was and writing blog posts to generate some website traffic.

But they never really built a demand generation engine that scaled pipeline faster, predictably.

The trade shows inevitably ended up working, to a degree. They met people, built connections, and closed some deals. The volume of deals didn't even matter. There was just enough pipeline to give the channel more attention.

This is why almost every B2B company goes to trade shows. It is also why far fewer B2B companies leverage Facebook Ads, for example. The barrier to entry is different. For trade shows, the barrier is finding a few events, getting a booth, and sending some marketing and sales team members down. For Facebook Ads, the barrier is figuring out how to target and attract the right prospect in a sea of infinite people that can be segmented in infinite ways.

That's not to say one is better than the other. Each has a place in the marketing strategy, depending on the company. Some should invest more heavily in trade shows. Some should invest more heavily in Facebook Ads.

The magic is in figuring out the right mix for each company. Understanding the specific business context is how you start to figure out the correct strategy for a particular company.

For Case Rocket, we had a starting point in knowing that Clio was in a similar market and had grown past $50 million in revenue with a massive marketing and sales budget. There were also several smaller players that made up the fragmented market of legal case management software who were actively investing more in marketing than Case Rocket.

What separated Case Rocket from these competitors, however, was the buyer they were focused on. Case Rocket's ideal customer was a midsize law firm, with 30 to 50 lawyers on staff. Clio, by contrast, had built the business by going after law firms with fewer than 20 lawyers. Other players in the space focused on the biggest law firms in the world to deliver a bespoke solution.

They were all selling a similar product, but each focused on a different segment. This had a huge impact on the Total Addressable Market (TAM) that Case Rocket was going after.

Clio's TAM was massive because there are hundreds of thousands of law firms that have 20 lawyers or fewer, especially when you factor in those run by solo practitioners. Clio's pricing reflected this reality, with a basic plan starting at $29 per month.

By contrast, there are less than 1,000 enterprise-level law firms that are multinational organizations. Pricing for solutions targeting this market ran well above $100,000 per year.

The disparity between pricing and TAM is interconnected.

A larger market often lends to a more transactional model where price points are lower and sales cycles are faster. A smaller market of enterprise customers leads to more customized solutions, which inevitably command a higher price.

Case Rocket was serving the market in the middle. Ocean-bridge ran a proper TAM analysis during the diligence process and found that Case Rocket had a serviceable market of about 60,000 law firms. That was still a sizable market but significantly smaller than Clio's. Case Rocket's pricing reflected this reality, with its average deal size coming in at about $30,000 a year.

"You can't beat Clio at Clio's game," I said to Janice, trying to set expectations. "You're actually not even playing the same game. Case Rocket's customers are larger in size and smaller in number. If you try to Go-To-Market the same way as Clio, you will lose. Instead, you need to play your own game by your own rules. That's how Case Rocket wins."

GUIDING DEMAND GENERATION PRINCIPLES

As we started to think about how Case Rocket could win its own share of customers in the legal case management software market, I introduced Janice to the concept of unlimited marketing budgets.

Budget, or lack thereof, is the biggest constrictor of creativity in the marketing function of most organizations. Because marketing leaders don't feel like additional budget will be approved, they don't even dream outside the established boundary of what they can spend.

"We need to think about this as if there were no budget restriction for Marketing," I said. "After all, you'd happily give Marketing as much budget as possible if it continued to generate revenue profitably, right?"

"Absolutely," Janice replied. "I want to give Marketing a lot more budget than it currently has because I know it has a lot more potential."

"I'm glad to hear that," I said. "The unlimited budget concept is a framework to think through the problem of how to scale Marketing. It doesn't mean we run a Super Bowl commercial just because there's money in the bank for it. It's more about figuring out all the possible ways to scale and then prioritizing them in the right order."

The truth is there is always more budget to go around. You just have to prove the ROI.

By removing the budget constraint, you can begin to think about all the avenues available to the business to scale its marketing efforts. You can then look at what budget each avenue requires and how much you are willing to fund.

This process allows you to always make your best, most profitable choices instead of potentially cutting off your best options before you even consider them.

MAPPING MARKETING TO THE CUSTOMER JOURNEY

The best place to start in mapping all your marketing opportunities with an unlimited budget is to map your ideal customer's journey from their perspective. Demand generation is less about convincing people to buy and more about meeting people where they are on their buyer journey.

Usually, that journey begins with a lack of awareness that there is a problem, followed by problem awareness, then a deeper and more thorough knowledge of potential solutions, and finally, consideration for a specific solution to purchase.

Unaware	Awareness	Knowledge	Consideration

As soon as you understand this concept, everything becomes about building content, assets, campaigns, and programs to meet prospects and buyers where they are on their journey. Then you can help them get to the next stage.

In Case Rocket's situation, prospects in the Consideration stage were likely booking demos with Janice's sales team and their competitors to evaluate what was best for them, while prospects in the Awareness stage may have been looking for content on how to save time with file management for law firms.

Case Rocket's marketing engine needed to fill these stages with experiences. Inevitably, there were gaps in the buyer journey where content was absent or below grade. The more Marketing could hold people's hands through this journey, the more likely prospects were to decide to purchase Case Rocket over its competitors.

When building the demand generation engine of a company from the ground up, there is not enough data to guide decisions. Case Rocket only had $300,000 in annual spend to analyze, and most of it was going into one channel. In situations like this, it's important to step beyond the limits of data analysis to focus on supporting the buyer journey with the right programs and campaigns.

In order to do this, it is helpful to understand the needs of customers at each stage of the journey.

Unaware	Awareness	Knowledge	Consideration
Needs to be made aware	Needs information	Needs nurturing and guidance	Needs to evaluate and make a decision

As you think about your marketing activities, you can easily map every marketing effort onto this continuum. For example, a PR campaign to get articles picked up by major legal publications is a broad awareness campaign focused on those who need information. The purpose of such a campaign is to simply move potential customers from unawareness to awareness. Conversely, a Google Ads campaign targeted at people looking for case management software is a late-funnel Consideration campaign for those who need to make a final decision on the product they want to purchase. The potential customer has enough awareness and knowledge already. The reach on this campaign would be a lot lower than the PR campaign, but the number of leads that come in would be a lot higher.

And they would be far more likely to close because as customers move through these stages, their intent increases.

Equally important is the fact that not all potential customers in each stage are equal. For example, a person who clicked a Google Ad for case management software is certainly in the Consideration stage, but they are not as close to buying from Case Rocket as someone who searches specifically for the term "Case Rocket." A person searching for a branded term has a higher affinity for the company and is thus most likely to buy from Case Rocket over its competitors.

Within the Consideration stage, each of those potential customers has a different level of interest—ranging from "cold" to "hot." Each prospect you encounter, then, has *both* an intent level and an interest level.

This is critically important to understand as you prepare to invest into marketing. If you build a framework for demand gen using only one of these dimensions, expensive mistakes will be made.

Combining interest with intent produces a framework that looks like this:

		INTENT	
	Awareness	Knowledge	Consideration
Hot	Needs expertise	Needs to know how software can solve a problem	Needs to test-drive the software
Warm	Needs frameworks	Needs to understand the problem	Needs to evaluate software options
Cold	Needs to answer a question	Needs a problem resolved	Needs software to solve a problem

INTEREST

Each of these "quadrants" addresses a particular customer need, from the very basic need to get a question answered all the way up to the need to test-drive your product before making that big purchase.

In practice, a company like Case Rocket may fill in its quadrants something like this:

	INTENT		
	Awareness	**Knowledge**	**Consideration**
Hot	Watches an educational webinar	Reads a case study	Ready for a free trial or demo
Warm	Downloads a content upgrade	Watches a software-focused webinar	Downloads a consumer guide
Cold	Reads an educational blog post	Reads an SEO blog post about software	Visits a marketing website and pricing page

(INTEREST axis on left)

Each marketing action directly relates to a customer need as well as their level of interest and intent. Developing an educational webinar answers a need for expertise from a prospect at the Awareness stage with hot interest. In the same way, developing a consumer guide will serve a prospect who needs to evaluate their software options and so is considering your product but has yet to heat up their interest to the point of purchasing from your particular company.

When we looked at demand generation this way, the gaps

in Case Rocket's assets, campaigns, and programs became very obvious:

- Someone in the Consideration/Cold stage is searching on Google for case management software. Was Case Rocket ranking for SEO or running paid advertising for those keywords? *No.*
- Someone in the Consideration/Warm stage needed a guide to compare case management software solutions against each other. Did Case Rocket have a guide that prospects could read to make their decision? *No.*
- Someone in the Consideration/Hot stage had booked a demo and asked a sales rep why they should choose Case Rocket over Clio. Did Case Rocket have battle cards for their sales reps to use? *No.*

Case Rocket was failing to support buyers on their journey and meet them where they were—at the most important moments in their journey. No wonder Janice felt like their Go-To-Market was not living up to its potential.

DOING THINGS IN THE RIGHT ORDER

"I feel like we don't have enough resources to execute on all of this," said Janice.

"You're right," I confirmed. "That's why we have to create an order of operations for your demand gen needs."

We started with putting an end to what wasn't working. Despite lacking the core assets above, Case Rocket had a team member writing weekly blog posts that no one was reading. It was a massive waste of time and resources, yet Case Rocket had been investing in it for years. It was a hamster wheel the marketing function could not stop running on.

This is one of the biggest mistakes made by marketing departments. They do things in random order when there are far more qualified prospects to build assets, campaigns, and programs for. To do things better means doing them in the right order.

Remember PEMDAS from mathematics class? That is the acronym for the order of operations when solving an equation: Parentheses first, then Exponents, Multiplication/Division, and finally Addition/Subtraction. Move left to right once all order matters are solved, and that gives you the answer.

Building a demand generation engine is very similar. The way we work left to right with PEMDAS, we work right to left and top to bottom in demand gen. Essentially, we work backward to arrive at which problem gets solved first:

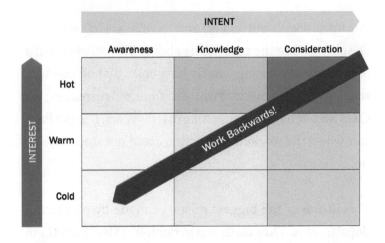

Each time an additional asset is created, more enterprise value is added to the business because more of the best prospects are being found, nurtured, and converted into real sales opportunities.

Instead of working in a random order on whatever demand gen opportunities present themselves on the day, Janice could now address each need in order, from the hottest prospects with the most intent backward.

PRIORITIZING OPPORTUNITY VERSUS INVESTMENT REQUIRED

Janice was ready to act.

"Let's start looking at budget and investing in reaching our hottest prospects."

"We still have to run this framework through your one final filter," I said. "Mapping opportunities versus investment required."

While order matters and working backward is critical, mapping opportunity versus investment tells us where we should really focus our initial demand gen energies. For example, to rank at the top of search results for "Case Management Software," Case Rocket could create an SEO asset that tries to rank organically, or it could simply pay to advertise for the keyword. This is where time and money are additional filters that decisions have to be made through.

An SEO asset that ranks for a highly competitive keyword like "Case Management Software" could take months to appear on the first page of Google. It would take effort to create the asset, optimize it, and promote it to get to that point. Conversely, a Google Ad for the same keyword could rank as the top result immediately, but it would take a monetary investment to get there.

The best place to start if you have the resources, then, is to advertise. You can get an immediate understanding of the potential impact of that campaign on your business. That is not to say the organic asset is not worth creating. It is just not the lowest-hanging fruit.

Once again, your strategy should be to work backward across the upper half of the grid.

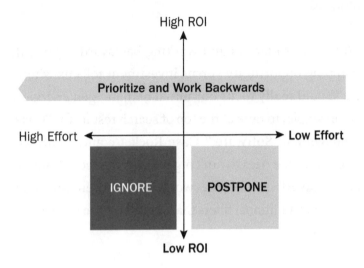

The key to success is balancing working backwards through both the customer journey and the opportunity versus effort framework. For example, a High-ROI/Low-Effort project in the Warm/Consideration stage may be more valuable to prioritize over a High ROI/High Effort project in the Hot/Consideration stage.

In Case Rocket's situation, after the Case Management software campaigns were launched, the next big opportunity was to focus on lists of identified target accounts that had engaged with the business and target them using LinkedIn, Facebook, and Instagram advertising. We didn't get to the organic assets until much later.

This doesn't mean you should avoid campaigns and channels that are difficult and valuable. But speed to outcomes is the best way to buy time and additional budget—particularly in those first 100 days. As demand and revenue scales and the board can see that, you are more likely to get more budget and resources to be able to address some of the high-investment opportunities.

This is where good judgment and decision-making are infinitely valuable.

CREATING DEMAND

As we took Case Rocket through this framework, demand skyrocketed. Within 18 months, the company grew from $7 million in revenue to over $12 million. Marketing pipeline was a big part of that story, growing by 350% during the same period while maintaining close rates.

Janice was overjoyed. She was already thinking about what to do next. "How do we scale this even more going forward?"

As companies like Case Rocket go through the frameworks in this chapter, they max out their potential marketing spend on channels that drive value for their business.

You can't spend an infinite amount on Google Ads for

people looking for 'Case Management Software' because there is a finite volume of those searches on a monthly basis.

That's where a lot of marketing organizations tap out. They enter a phase of predictable top-line revenue growth that is good enough, and so they are never incentivized to find that next gear.

"You've got to invest even more into content to create separation between yourself and your competitors," I explained to Janice.

The frameworks in this chapter initially had four buyer stages, but we never focused on people who are in the Unaware stage. The next gear involves helping prospects who are unaware discover that the market exists. Making them market-aware expands the category.

From an opportunity versus investment standpoint, these are the most expensive prospects to convert, and going after them before you max out all the other quadrants is not wise.

However, when you get to a point where you are capturing all the possible value from each stage and channel, this quadrant has the greatest amount of opportunity.

For Case Rocket, this meant emerging as the go-to destination for midsize law firms to come together and learn. They had to produce content at an astonishing rate. Janice began working on a book on how law firms can transition to the digital age. Case Rocket began hosting their own annual conference. They launched a podcast and YouTube channel. They began advertising on social media using videos and thought leadership content.

It was a market blitz. If you were a lawyer at a midsize law firm, there was no way you wouldn't eventually come across Case Rocket and become aware of their solution.

It took Janice and her team time to get there. They bought internal political capital by delivering on a number of demand gen initiatives and showing their impact on revenue. As time went on, the board approved more and more budget for marketing.

That's when it became a flywheel that kept turning. More growth led to more marketing budget, which led to more effective programs, which led to more growth. Once that flywheel reached a certain velocity, it couldn't be stopped. Case Rocket emerged as a dominant player in the Case Management software market.

All because Janice and her team did things in the right order.

3

CONTENT

*"There is no sale without the story;
no knockout without the setup."*

—GARY VAYNERCHUK

"We've already acquired three companies, with more in the pipeline," Martin told me. "Marketing needs to be able handle this complexity."

Martin was the CEO of SendLink, a leading sales enablement platform. Over the previous decade, SendLink had pioneered the sales enablement category along with its two biggest competitors, Seismic and Showpad. The industry had grown significantly in that time, and new competing platforms were emerging every day.

The market was fragmented, made up of many small players and a few eight-hundred-pound gorillas. In this kind of a market, SendLink's sponsor, Scorpion Capital, believed consolidation was the key to winning. Their view on the business was to acquire and integrate more of the smaller players to pick up a bigger portion of the market.

That's why, as soon as Scorpion invested in SendLink, it went on an acquisition spree and bought 3 other companies. It was Scorpion's standard playbook. Their entire portfolio was focused on making investments that involved rapid inorganic growth through M&A.

I'd worked with many of Scorpion Capital's companies before, so I knew exactly what to expect when I met Martin.

"We'll get this under control," I reassured him. Then I got to work.

Over the next couple of months, I dug into SendLink's marketing engine. I took the company through a due diligence process to understand Marketing's impact on revenue. We scaled channels that were doing well and worked through the demand gen framework to build the right roadmap for campaigns and programs.

As demand and pipeline started to ramp up, we encountered a major problem. A lot of leads were being generated, but they weren't converting to pipeline. Usually, when running through channel and campaign analysis, the right thing to do is to stop investing in places where the Acceptable Cost per MQL is too high, just like we did with Patricia and Cameron in chapter 1.

In SendLink's case, however, about $250,000 per month was being spent on paid media across all the product lines. Ad spend on Google was doing well, but paid social ads were suffering. A lot of leads from ideal customers in the right verticals were signing up for top-of-funnel offers. Many of these customers were from SendLink's target account list. They were good-fit leads. They just weren't converting.

The problem was that there was no supporting content to

nurture those leads through to opportunity status. That's when I turned my attention to the Content function.

I set a meeting with Toby, the Director of Content at Send-Link. Toby was an experienced content leader and had been in similar roles for almost 15 years. He had joined SendLink just a year ago, shortly before the sale to Scorpion went through.

"How are you deciding what content to create first?" I asked.

Toby gave me a blank stare.

I was asking because SendLink now had 16 product lines across 4 business units, which were collectively doing over $150 million in revenue. More acquisitions were going to happen every quarter, and there were limited content resources. There was a lot of content to create, so I wanted to know how the content team was prioritizing what was being worked on first.

"Right now we don't really have a method for prioritizing," stumbled Toby. "Most of our time is spent responding to requests from the sales team or supporting the M&A activity."

Given Toby's years of experience, he knew this wasn't a great answer. He was responsible for the content strategy of a massive company with multiple product lines, yet he didn't have a process for prioritizing what his team was working on.

A lot of SendLink's marketing performance was riding on his team's work, and Toby was running his team like an on-demand content marketing agency instead of a strategic, proactive function.

This wasn't his fault. When acquisitions happen at such a rapid clip, there is so much work to do. You need to support the acquisition and integration process; you need to support the sales team to hit its upsell and cross-sell targets; you need to drive more demand; and much more.

"Finding time to be strategic with content in this environment is not easy," I said empathetically. "But that's exactly what we need to do going forward."

"How do we do that?" he asked.

"By saying 'No' a lot more."

UNDERSTANDING CONTENT'S REALITY

Toby's content team faced the same challenge that almost every content team faces. Content is different from other functions in the organization—including other marketing areas like demand gen—because it has a major role to play at every stage of the customer journey. Sales comes in and works with qualified prospects to close new accounts or with existing customers to expand those accounts. Customer Success takes over onboarding and retention.

Content, on the other hand, is there for the entire journey. It plays a key part in how your customers move from Awareness to Activation to Adoption through to Advocacy.

Just think of all Content has to help you accomplish. It has to:

- Help you get discovered
- Nurture prospects and customers
- Enable the sales team to have better conversations
- Help customers get onboarded onto your platform
- Increase usage of your product
- Help cross-sell and upsell your other products to existing customers to capture white space opportunity
- Provide education to your customers to build loyalty, retention, and advocacy
- Build your brand as a publisher and thought leader in the marketplace

Each of these pillars likely requires a dedicated team. Yet Content is almost always understaffed and underfunded.

As a result, the content team's work inevitably becomes reactive.

Inside SendLink's rapid M&A expansion environment, this reactivity was amplified. There were more product lines to support and board-level expectations for Content to support the acquisition and integration process. At the same time, content was needed to ramp up demand generation to hit aggressive sales targets.

That's why Toby's position was not an enviable one.

His strategy to deliver, as best as he could, was to acquiesce to the demands of the sales team. After all, if Sales is requesting a piece of content to help them close a deal, that should get the highest priority, right?

Sometimes yes. Sometimes the best way for Content to make an impact is by enabling the sales team to close more deals in the pipeline.

But not always.

Sometimes, Content has higher priorities. They just can't see them because of the seeming urgency of the overwhelming number of requests they have coming in. When Content puts those higher priorities aside, the whole company suffers.

For SendLink, the cost of poor content prioritization was coming in the form of lead volume that was not converting to pipeline and revenue. Toby was delivering on all the sales enablement and corporate marketing content he needed to create, but he was falling short on the revenue side of what the organization needed from Content.

What confuses content leaders like Toby in an environment like SendLink's is that they mix up productivity with value creation. Backlog builds up, and most of it is categorized as urgent because it has to get done by a certain time. Press releases for acquisitions have to go out. An updated sales resource is needed for a meeting. A rebranding project to integrate new acquisitions involves changing all the website assets.

This is all urgent work. It is also a lot of busywork. Meanwhile, the pipeline needed for SendLink to reach its projections suffers.

I've seen a lot of marketers make this mistake. I've seen them go all-in on a rebranding project as part of integrating new acquisitions and lose their job 10 months later because there wasn't enough pipeline. I've seen board meetings turn into disastrous, career-hampering moments for marketing executives because they focused on juggling short-term priorities instead of creating enterprise value.

I wasn't going to let Toby make the same mistake.

"There's just so much to manage," Toby said, overwhelmed. "How do I focus Content on doing it all?"

"It's a lot more manageable than it initially seems," I said. "We just need to build a system so you are always working on the most valuable piece of content for the company."

BUILDING A CONTENT ROADMAP

Content is a lot like Product Management. Product Management constantly faces requests from every aspect of the organization. Sales wants features that will help them overcome objections and close deals. Customer Success wants features that will help them onboard, expand, and retain accounts. UX wants usability improvements. Support wants bug fixes.

The list of what Product Management needs to sift through is endless. The only difference is that Product Management is a far more mature function in organizations and has had the time to develop best practices.

Product Management teams use Agile methodologies, have robust backlogs, and constantly reprioritize what enters into their workstream based on the demands of their organization and what will create the most value for the business.

Doesn't this sound a lot like what Toby and his Content organization needed to do?

"We want Content to be focused on the items that deliver the most ROI," I said to Toby. "With so many different inputs for what Content can be producing, it is critical to have a prioritization mechanism—a content roadmap."

Over the next month, Toby and I worked together to build the content roadmap for SendLink, using a step-by-step process.

First, we took an inventory of all of SendLink's existing content. The inventory categorized all content against the following dimensions:

- Product line
- Funnel stage
- Use case
- Campaign
- Geography
- Vertical
- Persona
- Content type
- Status

The goal of the inventory was to audit what already existed and understand SendLink's biggest gaps in content.

Second, we prioritized the biggest opportunity areas based on ROI. To do this, we had to see where the revenue was being lost.

By analyzing Toby's funnel data for one product line, we found that $70,000 was being spent per month that was generating about 120 MQLs, which was a success at a Cost per MQL level based on SendLink's historical data. From that initial 120 MQLs, though, only 13 made it to opportunity status, a conversion rate of 11%. Out of those 13 Opportunities, 4 deals closed, at an average deal size of $12,000.

SendLink was closing about 30% of its opportunities. Those 4 deals generated $48,000 in revenue on $70,000 in ad spend. In a lot of companies, that's not terrible performance. Generating $0.68 in revenue for every $1 in marketing spend is a decent return. It means you're breaking even by about month 15. Closing 30% of opportunities is also a strong win rate.

The problem was the conversion from MQL to Opportunity. Generating 120 MQLs for $70,000 meant that SendLink's Cost per MQL was $583. For a company with an average deal size of $12,000, this was a very good place to be. However, with only 13 opportunities generated from those 120 MQLs, SendLink's Cost per Opportunity skyrocketed to $5,400.

Spend	$70,000
MQLs	120
Opportunities	13
MQL to Opp Rate	11%
Cost/Opportunity	$5,400
Closed Won	4
Close Rate	31%
Average Deal Size	$12,000
Total Revenue	$48,000

This implied that SendLink needed to close 50% of Opportunities to break even within a year, which was unlikely, despite having a healthy sales motion in place. However, if SendLink could increase its 11% conversion rate from MQL to Opportunity to 20%, it would imply that the number of Opportunities from the same number of MQLs would increase to 24. It would also imply that 7 deals would close instead of 4 from the same investment, which would lead to $84,000 in revenue for the initial investment of $70,000.

In other words, Content's highest ROI work was to

strengthen the middle of the funnel, where most of the leads were being lost. That was just the data for 1 product line, but as we went through the rest, we found similar issues: it was always the middle of the funnel where they were losing leads.

Every company's content challenge is different. Are you getting a good number of opportunities, but they're not converting to Closed Won deals at a high enough rate? Or are you generating lots of traffic that isn't translating to lots of MQLs?

This is why running a diagnostic is the key to figuring out which area content teams should focus on. Without a proper audit of where content resources are best allocated, Content is more reactive than data-driven.

The stage of your funnel that needs extra support suggests which types of content you should prioritize.

- If you're not getting enough leads to keep your sales team busy, prioritize top-of-funnel content, such as SEO content and email-capture assets.
- If early-stage leads are getting stuck in the marketing pipeline and failing to convert to SQLs, prioritize the middle-of-the-funnel content, such as nurture programs.
- If opportunities are converting into customers at a low

rate, prioritize sales enablement content, such as decks and battle cards.

- If customers are not renewing or not using the product in an optimal way, prioritize product marketing and customer success content—for example, a customer newsletter and product webinars.

Third, Toby and I prioritized content roadmap items across product lines.

In environments like Toby's, where acquisitions are a core part of the business strategy, complexity increases with each acquisition. As complexity increases, these gaps are more difficult to spot.

Asking the following questions helps narrow down which assets need to be prioritized over others:

- Which product line has the most value to the business?
- Which product line has the most growth potential, especially if supported by content?
- Which product line is core to the success of other product lines? (This is especially true in platform companies where 1 product is the core business, while others are extensions.)

In Toby's case, SendLink's core platform accounted for 80% of revenue despite the rapid M&A strategy. The acquisitions were primarily add-ons and bolt-ons to SendLink's core business. Toby's content roadmap needed to account for this reality, even if it meant not addressing certain gaps across other product lines.

By the end of this 3-step process, Toby and his content team had a roadmap sorted by priority and impact on the business. Of course, there were still some judgment calls to make. But Toby finally had a prioritization mechanism that allowed his content organization to be more proactive and strategic than reactive.

SCALING CONTENT WITH PEOPLE

"I wish we had done this right after the acquisition by Scorpion," Toby lamented. "I was spinning my wheels for months before we built this roadmap together."

The work we had done was a one-time, front-loaded investment that changed how Toby's team operated. From then on, they were laser-focused on where Content was going to add value.

There was a clear content roadmap in place, and Martin and the executive team were fully aware of the why behind what content was working on.

As sales enablement requests came in, Toby's team pushed

them to the backlog and continued to stay on track. Other than the necessary communications related to new acquisitions, Toby's team stayed on the course of strengthening the middle of the funnel. In a few months, they had transformed the customer journey for leads coming in at the top of the funnel, and we started to see the impact of the work on revenue.

Conversions from MQL to Opportunity increased from 11% to 13%, then to 15%, then to 18%. Twelve months later, SendLink was converting 25% of its MQLs into Opportunities. Costs per Opportunity plummeted, revenue from top of funnel campaigns increased significantly, and SendLink was able to spend a lot more to acquire leads.

Martin was so happy with the progress that we stayed on retainer to support SendLink's marketing organization through 4 other acquisitions. As the acquisitions ramped up, the same problem kept coming up. Each time, Toby and I would run through the same process, and each time, trade-offs had to be made to prioritize the biggest opportunity areas.

With so many product lines, however, there was always one good opportunity being sacrificed for a better one. Even with a great roadmap and prioritization framework in place, Toby's team was falling behind.

"We can't keep up with the volume," said Toby. "We are drowning in the amount of content needed to capture all the opportunities available across the business."

"This is why prioritization and roadmapping will only get you so far," I responded. "It's time to focus on scaling with people."

TEAM

*"Great vision without great
people is irrelevant."*

—JIM COLLINS

"I don't see a cohesive marketing strategy for our organization," said Stuart.

"What's missing?" I asked, trying to piece the situation together.

"I don't see a clear plan from Marketing on how we will find customers in this market beyond traditional channels," he responded.

Stuart was the CEO of Enerscope, a platform focused on helping companies in the oil and gas industry find major cost efficiencies in their supply chain. When Zenith Capital invested in Enerscope, they did a full market segmentation analysis and found that Enerscope had a serviceable market of only 1,725 customers in the oil and gas industry. Of those 1,725 targets, 647 were ideal fits.

It was a clearly defined market, and it was small. The market opportunity, however, was sizable. Enerscope's pricing started at $150,000 and scaled north of $400,000 per account. These were all whales. Getting into the account meant the customer was staying with Enerscope for 10 or more years, so their Lifetime Value was north of $2 million on average.

Despite this kind of market opportunity, leads were only being generated from two channels: trade shows and outbound sales calls. That definitely made sense to some degree. Given the high deal values, sales cycles were long, and you had to build relationships with customers to sell them over time.

In this reality, Marketing's primary contribution came from the annual conference Enerscope held for its customers and prospects. The conference, OAGX, was generating 80% of the marketing-generated pipeline for the business. For a company that was doing $70 million in revenue like Enerscope, this was a major source of risk.

"We're so reliant on OAGX, we haven't built a proper strategy to go after this market beyond trade shows," said Stuart. "We need a better plan."

Stuart was convinced his marketing organization needed to rethink its strategy if Enerscope was ever going to have a chance of hitting its targets.

I sat down with Kristin, the VP of Marketing at Enerscope, to understand how her team was thinking about scaling their Marketing.

"Most of our efforts go into planning OAGX," Kristin told me. "It takes all year."

"What about marketing beyond OAGX?" I asked. I wanted

to see what other activities were going into pipeline generation.

"We're doing some work beyond that in areas like sales enablement and product marketing," she responded. "To be honest, there isn't enough time or resources to do more. We know we need to. We just don't have the bandwidth."

Kristin's five-person marketing team was executing on only one major demand generation program a year. While there was a significant amount of pipeline generated from that one event, the sales organization at Enerscope was always in feast or famine mode.

When I asked Brad, VP of Sales at Enerscope, for his thoughts on OAGX, he didn't pull any punches.

"It's frustrating," he said. "The whole year we're asking Marketing to run more demand generation programs, and what we hear back is that they're too busy with OAGX. They're actually planning OAGX for next year right now, and this year's conference is still months away."

The sales team was operating alone for three out of the four quarters of the year, doing cold outreach as their main mechanism for scaling demand. There was a lot of angst in the organization about the role of OAGX. The marketing team felt like it was doing a great job, but the rest of the organization felt they weren't getting enough support.

As the landscape became clearer to me, I went back to Stuart and gave him my diagnosis. "Your marketing team doesn't have enough people," I said. "In fact, you need to restructure your entire marketing organization."

"I don't understand," Stuart responded. "I thought the point of our engagement with you was to figure out the marketing strategy."

"It is," I responded. "But there aren't enough people on the team. That's why there isn't a marketing strategy. Kristen is doing a great job with Corporate Marketing and Events, but she needs more support. Some key roles are missing.

"Demand generation is suffering because your marketing team is focused entirely on OAGX," I continued. "They're focusing there not because there isn't opportunity elsewhere but because it takes a lot of resources to deliver on that conference."

I walked Stuart through what a new organizational structure would look like. He needed multiple roles filled. He needed a Director of Demand Generation who would focus on ABM strategies to target the 1,725 customers identified in the market segmentation analysis and experiment with new channels to generate pipeline. He needed a Content leader and two content specialists who would execute on the content roadmap to support demand generation initiatives, OAGX, sales enablement, and more. He needed a paid media agency to ramp up digital demand generation campaigns.

To accomplish all that, he would need to invest in more marketing resources to support the additional structure. The additional investment would allow Kristen to operate like the true VP of Marketing the business needed to lead the overall marketing strategy and organization.

"That's a lot of additional investment into headcount," Stuart said, mulling it over. "What if we miss our targets after investing all this money?"

"You're much more likely to miss if you don't," I responded.

UNDERSTANDING THE KEY MARKETING FUNCTIONS

While each company has a unique context, the roles Marketing requires to succeed at scale have a lot of alignment across organizations. Some companies rely heavily on events and require a bigger events team, while others rely heavily on digital and require more demand generation specialists. Regardless, the underlying structure that the company needs to build toward remains largely the same.

Each marketing department needs the following functions, with the number of roles varying based on the context of the company.

1. Corporate—Covering the Brand, Communications, and PR responsibilities that are required to scale a company, especially in an M&A environment
2. Events—Organizing and running in-person or virtual events and trade shows that drive pipeline through relationships and require a lot of coordination
3. Product Marketing—Interfacing with Product teams to understand key benefits of features and products and communicating that to new and existing customers
4. Customer Marketing—Creating campaigns to cross-sell and upsell existing customers on additional products and services
5. Sales Enablement—Supporting the sales team with collateral, thought leadership, and content to help them close more deals
6. Content Marketing—Building all the assets necessary to support the buyer and customer journey from awareness to nurture content, consideration, and beyond
7. Demand Generation—Investing in programs and campaigns on digital and offline channels to drive pipeline
8. Marketing Operations—Aligning the entire marketing function with data to understand ROI on marketing spend so that Marketing can scale faster

Notice that none of the functions are restricted to a channel or tactic. There isn't a "Google Ads" function or an "Account-Based Marketing" function or an "SEO" function. Each of those are specifics within the bigger buckets of the function. For some companies, ABM will be the primary demand gen avenue. For others, digital paid advertising will be better. Regardless of the particular requirements of your company, they should all fall into one demand gen function.

In small companies, 2 to 3 people can fulfill all of these functions. At scale—for example, inside large companies with 12,000-plus employees, like Intuit—these 8 functions can have hundreds of people inside, each with distinct roles to support broader marketing goals. The key is to figure out where a company is along that spectrum and staff up accordingly.

Budget does not have to be equally distributed between the functions. In some companies, Sales Enablement gets the bulk of the budget. In others, Content Marketing has the heaviest investment.

The specifics of each organization determine how much budget each function receives. That's why it is important to think of each function as a collection of roles. The roles inside each function can be filled by one person or twenty—and receive half the budget or a twentieth—depending on the scale and strategy of the company.

In Enerscope's case, the team leaned heavily toward events and corporate marketing and not nearly enough toward content and demand generation. That's why the new structure required new leaders for each of those functions, with additional resources underneath.

SCALING MARKETING TEAMS

Figuring out the specific needs of a particular marketing organization starts with self-awareness. Where is the overall organization on its journey and what does it need from Marketing at this current stage?

Regardless of industry, company, or product, there are 4 key stages of scaling marketing organizations.

STAGE 1: STARTUP

The term "startup" is not just limited to small companies here. In this context, it can also refer to companies that have never really invested in Marketing. Inside these companies, there is usually a marketing team of 1 to 3 people. These are junior marketers and supporting cast members. In most cases, small marketing teams are focused on supporting sales efforts more than making marketing a revenue driver. You'll most often find this team in a company doing less than $5 million in revenue or an enterprise B2B company where Sales is the star.

This stage is actually where Enerscope's marketing team was, despite the fact that the company was doing $70 million in revenue. With average deal sizes of $150,000 or more, the marketing team never got the funding or influx of marketing expertise it needed to scale.

STAGE 2: FINDING SCALE

These marketing organizations are transitioning into becoming revenue generators and have 1 or 2 senior managers leading a team of 7 or 8 people. They are building the systems, processes, and operational structure required to scale Marketing's revenue impact. Sales and Marketing begin to work more closely together at this stage because the marketing team needs feedback from Sales on the quality of the pipeline it is driving. You'll most often find this team inside a company doing $5 million to $15 million in revenue.

This was the next stage of evolution for Enerscope's marketing team: more demand gen and more revenue accountability with more resources to be able to deliver on that accountability.

STAGE 3: GROWTH

At this stage, marketing organizations have figured out channels and campaigns that drive revenue and are focused on scaling. There is an operational structure in place, there are many marketers on the team, and 3 or 4 leaders. The team size by this point is usually north of 15. Marketing and Sales operate as peers and have an equal seat at the table.

They are also often funded equally well. You'll most often find this team in a company that is doing at least $20 million to $50 million in revenue.

This is the stage of high-performing marketing teams, and it has largely been the focus of this book to help your company reach it. This is also where I wanted to take Enerscope and where I want to take all How To SaaS clients.

STAGE 4: MULTIPRODUCT, MULTINATIONAL

This marketing organization is most commonly found inside an M&A environment where you have $100 million-plus companies that are a combination of multiple product lines doing different amounts of revenue. Inorganic growth is the main strategy to drive enterprise value. These marketing organizations vary in size and investment. Often, they have more than 25 team members dispersed across the different product lines. The team is likely also dispersed across regions, targeting customers in different languages—for example, having a Latin American or European team is not all that uncommon.

In teams like this, you have the challenge of selling different products priced at different price points to different markets. You have cross-sell targets to hit to existing customers along with your net new targets. The complexity level is high.

We encountered a company at this stage in the last chapter in SendLink. Like SendLink, organizations sometimes find themselves at this stage before they've gone through the previous stages. In Enerscope's case, for example, Stuart and Zenith Capital were working on scaling up M&A activities to buy 2 companies. Once those acquisitions came in, Enerscope's marketing team would have moved to this stage before it had navigated going through the evolution of the previous stages.

Being in this position is incredibly risky. If you grow faster than the people side of your organization can handle, the likely outcome is failure to meet expectations. That's why ramping up marketing maturity needs to happen in parallel.

IDENTIFYING CRITICAL GAPS

As complexity increases, so will your team needs as you scale through the stages. At Stage 1, hiring a Marketing Director can make all the difference. At Stage 4, you need multiple marketing leads who report to a seasoned CMO. Spend and budgets change; revenue targets change.

At each stage, there are different expectations to hit as well. Take the role of Marketing Operations leader, for example, which is tasked with helping you make sense of all the different places Marketing is investing budget and how it is performing. You can certainly move along without a Marketing Operations Lead in Stage 2. However, when you get to Stage 4, your entire survival depends on having that role filled.

This is not just about the stage. Depending on the company, the critical gaps are different. Some companies are stronger at demand gen, while others are strong at product marketing. No company will be a leader in all 8 areas of marketing defined above, nor is it necessary for the company to be good at everything.

The level of complexity at SendLink (from chapter 3) required building a more mature Content function that could prioritize across multiple product lines. Case Rocket, from chapter 2, needed to build the foundation for scaling demand generation by working backward through their biggest opportunities. Pass Spring, in chapter 1, needed to set up the right accountability framework for marketing. Fleetsync, in the introduction, needed to get its data in order.

And Enerscope needed to build a demand generation program focused on ABM to target its defined market of 1,725 accounts.

An enterprise B2B company needs more marketers that understand Account-Based Marketing. A high-velocity, low-ACV SaaS company needs more inbound marketers to create content and run demand gen programs.

Every company is different.

This is why understanding where you are as a company and what kind of marketing team you need is the key to success. It is also why you need to map your gaps back to the investment thesis.

GETTING BUDGET FOR HIRING

As I walked Stuart through the above framework, he started to see all the gaps in the marketing organization. Six out of the eight marketing functions were not being done well, if at all, at Enerscope. The marketing team was stuck in the Startup phase and busy running on the hamster wheel of delivering on OAGX. There weren't enough leaders on the team and not enough expertise. That's why they never stopped to ask what else the organization needed.

At Enerscope's next board meeting with Zenith, Stuart's presentation walked his board through the challenges with marketing-generated pipeline and the overreliance on OAGX. Stuart then made a recommendation to scale the marketing organization to add several more key roles, so that Enerscope could begin scaling demand generation beyond OAGX. To do that, he explained, he'd need more budget.

The board was acutely aware of the risks associated with being so reliant on OAGX and had wanted this problem solved for a while. They were thrilled to hear the recommendation, and the budget was approved without hesitation.

Now that we had the green light, Stuart and I could move beyond conceptualizing the challenge and begin to truly transform the marketing organization.

INVESTMENT COMMITTEE

"We have three baskets for investing: yes, no, and too difficult to understand."

—CHARLIE MUNGER

"I can't go to the board with my marketing team's budget recommendations," said Sam. "If I'm not satisfied with my VP of Marketing's explanation, I know the board won't be."

Sam was the CEO of Schedule Desk, a field service management software for contractors. It was a massive, horizontal market because every kind of contractor needed a tool like Schedule Desk to run the day-to-day operations of their business. That's what powered Schedule Desk's growth to $17 million in revenue in less than 4 years.

In most markets, such progress is unheard of. To go from founding a company to anything north of $10 million is an incredible achievement. It shows the customer validation of the product and the size of the market opportunity. That's why Jetstream Equity moved quickly to acquire the business within a couple of months.

"I've got a board meeting coming up in December," continued Sam. "I need you to work with Melissa and help make a recommendation on the right-sized budget for Marketing by that meeting. My gut says we're going to need to be a lot more aggressive with our budget ask for Marketing, but I need to validate that."

Melissa was Schedule Desk's VP of Marketing. She had been in the organization since the beginning. She started as a marketing coordinator and slowly built the function as the business grew. Eventually, Sam promoted her to VP when he needed to shore up his executive team for the acquisition talks. So she knew the organization inside and out.

"Our competition is killing us right now," said Melissa when I first met her. "They're outspending us on marketing by 2 to 3 times."

Melissa wasn't wrong. Schedule Desk was operating in a fast-growing market with some major competitors. Jobber and ServiceTitan were two of the biggest names in the industry and were spending a lot more than Schedule Desk across the board. They had larger marketing teams, significantly bigger paid media budgets, and were publishing way more content.

Meanwhile, Melissa's marketing team was a total of 6 people, and her entire marketing budget was $900,000. She was spending $600,000 of that budget on programs, which would have been a decent amount in most markets, but not this one. There was so much competition and so much market opportunity to capture.

"Let me ask you one thing," I said. "How have you asked for more budget?" I wanted to know what went into the budget she had presented to Sam.

"I took our current marketing spend and increased it by 30% for next year," said Melissa. "Then I broke down that increased spend between different channels and headcount."

"Where did the 30% increase come from?" I inquired further.

"It was my rough estimate of what we need to get to the same spending levels as Jobber and ServiceTitan," responded Melissa.

I now had a clearer understanding of Sam's hesitation in giving Melissa additional budget. She had a good understanding of the market, she knew she had to spend more to scale, and so she had asked for more marketing budget as a result.

The only problem was that she had made a critical budgeting mistake. She was treating budgeting more like a math exercise than a strategic one. She had no underlying data to back up her budget ask.

"Your instinct to ask for more budget for marketing looks right to me," I said, validating Melissa's thinking. "You have raw instincts from watching the business grow over 4 years. You can sense what needs to be done by just reading the market landscape."

"Why does Sam think the budget won't get approved, then?" Melissa asked, puzzled.

"Because data is your board's native language," I explained. "And you haven't translated your budget ask into that language."

UNDERSTANDING BOARD DECISIONS

What I needed to get Melissa to wrap her head around was that the board is always willing to fund opportunities that generate ROI.

As we discussed in the unlimited budget exercise, a lot of marketing leaders believe it's a losing battle to ask for more budget. This is often the case in organizations that are Sales-led, where Marketing is viewed as a cost center. These marketing leaders resign themselves to sticking to roughly the same budget year after year because they believe the board won't approve additional budget.

While there is some truth to it, this thinking requires adjustment. It's more accurate to say that the board will always refuse to fund increases in Marketing budget until it has the data to understand why that additional budget is necessary.

The reality of investors and boards is that every department inside every portfolio company wants more budget. Sales wants more reps, Product wants more designers, Engineering wants more engineers, and Marketing wants more ad spend.

In this situation, trade-offs have to be made, and opportunity costs are always at stake. For example, should the board give marketing another $1 million in budget or hire 10 sales people to generate more revenue? Should they hire 2 engineers to address our product roadmap or 2 product marketers to communicate about our product with customers? Should they hire a Director of Demand Generation or another Product Manager?

These are very difficult decisions to make. CEOs like Sam end up being a filter for budget asks like Melissa's. Part of the CEO's job is to work with the CFO to bring together the budget asks of all the departments and decide what mix of investments to pitch to the board.

A board meeting is high-stakes poker. There is scrutiny on every side and every recommendation. If things don't work out, the CEO is ultimately accountable for what was presented.

This is why Melissa asking for a 30% increase in budget on gut feel was not good enough for Sam. He needed to have more confidence in the marketing plan and increased budget.

ALIGNING WITH BOARD TARGETS (TOP-DOWN)

The likelihood of getting an increased amount of budget approved drastically increases if Marketing can do two things: first, tie its budget ask to what has already been forecasted for revenue. And second, show where that investment will pay off.

For Melissa, answering this first point meant going through the entire marketing due diligence process and understanding Schedule Desk's conversion rates throughout the funnel. As we looked across all channels, we uncovered that about 10% of MQLs were becoming opportunities, and about 40% of opportunities became Closed Won deals. This meant roughly 4% of MQLs were becoming Closed Won deals. Every time Melissa and her team generated 25 MQLs, 1 deal would close.

With an annual contract value of $25,000, this meant Schedule Desk had an Acceptable Cost per MQL of $1,000 to have a payback period of less than 12 months. Some channels were more expensive than others, but that was the blended baseline Melissa's team needed to shoot for.

"Now let's look at our board projections for next year," I told Melissa. "How many new customers does the business need to generate from marketing activities?"

Melissa went through the latest projections put together by

Schedule Desk's CFO. The company was expected to grow from $17 million in revenue to $21 million in the next year. Of that additional $4 million in growth, $2.5 million was tied to landing new customers, while the rest was tied to other strategic initiatives. Marketing needed to generate 80% of that revenue, meaning it had to generate $2 million in bookings.

At an annual contract value of $25,000, this meant that Melissa's team needed to generate 80 deals in the next 12 months. Those 80 deals needed 200 opportunities, based on Schedule Desk's historical conversion rates. To generate those 200 opportunities, Melissa's team needed to generate 2,000 MQLs.

At an Acceptable Cost per MQL of $1,000, this meant that Melissa's team needed a Marketing Budget of $2 million! This was more than double Melissa's budget of $900,000 the year before. Even if the board had agreed to Melissa's ask of a 30% increase, that would have only gotten her a budget of $1.17 million.

Historically, Schedule Desk had been closing about $1 million in new bookings each year. The marketing budget of $900,000 in that environment was set closer to where it needed to be. When board projections rapidly increased, however, a matching adjustment on the underlying activities to meet those projections did not occur.

This was the story Melissa needed to tell Sam and the board.

"This is a shared problem," I said. "When you and Sam show the board all this data, you're giving them the right information to be able to solve this problem together."

ALLOCATING BUDGET TO MARKETING OPPORTUNITIES (BOTTOM-UP)

This was a great step forward for Melissa, but there was more work to do. Before Melissa could take the gap in the Marketing budget to Sam, she needed to figure out where Schedule Desk could invest more marketing budget confidently. Asking for $1.1 million in additional budget sounded great, but she needed to show the board a clear path to meeting its sales projections.

We began by analyzing Melissa's current channels of marketing spend to understand which channels were performing better than others. Within those channels, Google Ads, LinkedIn Ads, Facebook Ads, and Content were performing really well for Schedule Desk.

On Google Ads, Melissa's team was spending $20,000 per month. It was her team's biggest channel of spend. The ROI on the channel was phenomenal, as the cost per MQL was less than $800 for many campaigns. Even better, those that were performing particularly well had a lot more room to scale—up to 300%. There were a few campaigns that were spending a lot more than $2,000 per MQL, and those were immediately stopped.

Scalability on Facebook and LinkedIn was even better. Schedule Desk was only spending $3,000 per month between those 2 channels, and there was room to scale it by 10 times or more.

Schedule Desk was also producing a lot of content already. But with an MQL to Opportunity conversion rate of 10%, there was a lot of work to do to increase the number of leads that got through to Opportunity status. This required personalized content for every industry, persona, use case, and vertical. Given that Schedule Desk was such a horizontal platform, this work was essential to driving conversion rates through the funnel.

Between all of these opportunities, there was a lot more that Marketing could have been doing to reach Schedule Desk's revenue projections. The urgency of doing this work was high because those projections would be missed if this marketing work was not prioritized.

In mapping the opportunities, Melissa and I came up with a summarized plan for paid media that looked like the following:

Marketing Program	Current Annual Spend	Adjusted Annual Spend	Additional Revenue
Scale Google Ads	$240,000	$750,000	$500,000
Scale Facebook and LinkedIn Ads	$36,000	$300,000	$300,000

Using data, Melissa asked for an additional $774,000 for paid media and promised additional revenue of $800,000 from the channels involved based on the analysis we worked on together.

For Content, the summary looked a little different:

Funnel Stage	Conversion Rates and Values	Adjusted Rates and Values	Additional Revenue	Additional Spend
MQL	10% (25 MQLs)	20% (12.5 MQLs)	$500,000	$100,000 (2 hires)
Opportunity	40% (2.5 Opps)	40% (2.5 opps)		
Closed Won	$25,000 (1 deal)	$25,000 (1 deal)		

The pitch for giving Content more budget was to signal that funnel conversion rates would improve if more resources could focus on creating content to support the buyer journey further. The cost wasn't program spend, it was headcount.

Melissa also needed additional headcount beyond the content hires. Her team of 6 people was full of junior marketers. Melissa did not have any senior direct reports who could help her scale to the level of expectations required. In order to do this, she needed a Director of Demand Generation, a Paid Media agency, and a Director of Content to run her bigger content team.

Between all of these investments, Melissa's marketing budget increased to $2.1 million. She summarized her asks to the board as follows:

Investment Area	Additional Revenue	Additional Revenue	Priority Level
Scale Paid Media	$800,000	$774,000	High
Scale Middle-of-Funnel Content	$500,000		High
Two Content Marketers		$100,000	High
Hire Director of Demand Gen		$120,000	High
Hire Head of Content		$100,000	Medium
Hire Paid Media Agency		$100,000	Medium
TOTAL	$1,300,000	$1,194,000	

Melissa was asking for a marketing budget of $2.1 million, more than double her previous marketing budget of $900,000. It was a significant ask, to put it mildly.

"I'm nervous," said Melissa. "I feel like I'm going to be laughed out of the room for asking for something so egregious."

"It's not egregious," I said. "You are a steward of the business, bringing data to the table and showing a clear path to achieve shared objectives. That's the language the board wants to have its conversations in."

PRESENTING YOUR BUDGET ASK

Sam was over the moon when Melissa showed him what we had come up with.

"This is exactly what I was looking for," said Sam. "I knew you weren't asking for enough budget, Melissa. This story and budget ask sounds a lot more like something we can sell to the board."

Sam was right. Had Melissa gone with her ask of a 30% increase to the board, she would have been unlikely to get it. Even if she had, she would have still missed her targets and likely lost her job, and the business would have suffered as a result. Asking for the right amount of budget and using the language the board speaks meant that Melissa was far more likely to succeed and hit those targets.

Sam and Melissa prepared over a few sessions and finally presented the updated ask at the next board meeting. As expected, Melissa got every dollar of additional marketing investment she was looking for.

Over the next 12 months, Marketing became more efficient,

generated more demand, and improved conversion rates through the funnel. Melissa had a bigger team and more marketing budget than ever before.

And Schedule Desk crushed its sales projections.

CONCLUSION

"Compound interest is the eighth wonder of the world."

—ALBERT EINSTEIN

All the stories in this book involve different companies, CEOs, marketing leaders, and investors facing different challenges. But they're also, in many ways, the same story.

Henry needed to know the truth about marketing's impact on revenue with data so he could show North Star Capital how he was going to meet Fleetsync's ambitious growth projections.

Cameron and Patricia needed to understand how much they could scale marketing for Pass Spring after spending $1 million on LinkedIn ads and not tracking impact on Closed Won deals.

Janice needed to build a data-driven go-to-market strategy for Case Rocket in a competitive market and figure out where to allocate additional marketing investments.

Martin and Toby needed to figure out how Content could help SendLink scale its multiproduct business in an M&A environment, and how many resources were necessary to deliver.

Stuart and Kristin needed to drive growth from Marketing beyond their annual conference and needed to invest in the right roles and people to do it.

Sam and Melissa needed to get approval for more than

double their marketing budget to execute on the growth plans the business needed to deliver on.

When you zoom out, each story has the same components. Each had a company that needed to scale faster. Each needed to scale Marketing to do it. And each needed better organization and more Marketing budget to get there.

This is the same story we encounter with our clients every day at How To SaaS. We've seen variations of the exact same story thousands of times.

And the solution to the problem can be summarized in one word: Data.

Marketing needs more data to understand and scale its impact on revenue. Increased impact on revenue leads to more budget. More budget gives Marketing the ability to make an even greater impact on revenue.

Each time Marketing goes through this framework, it emerges with an even greater ability to make an impact on revenue because it helps everyone win. Marketing leaders win because they get more budget, get taken more seriously, and emerge as true executives inside organizations. Other departments win because Marketing becomes a true partner in revenue. CEOs win because their companies scale faster and hit their projections. Investors win because their investment theses are proved out and their investments grow.

The need to follow this framework is amplified post-acquisition, when the urgency to create enterprise value in the first 100 days becomes even more important.

With heightened expectations, all stakeholders are trying to figure out where they can use money as fuel to turn their investments into a rocket ship. In these scenarios, investors and boards are eager to invest even more into Marketing to scale the business faster.

To succeed, Marketing needs to come prepared with the right data to every board meeting. There needs to be a disciplined cadence inside companies to follow this framework on at least an annual basis, and ideally quarterly. CEOs need to use the framework to hold their marketing leaders accountable, while boards need to use the framework to understand how much budget to allocate to Marketing.

This framework, if followed religiously, compounds over time. Even if a company is Sales-led and doesn't give Marketing enough budget to start, following this framework ensures that Marketing gets a bigger seat at the table as time goes on and is eventually a true rainmaker in the organization.

If you are a CEO, investor, or executive who wants to take your company's marketing function to the next level, schedule a consult at www.howtosaas.com to see how we can help your business scale faster.

RESOURCES

Each chapter in this book has a set of frameworks and templates that you can use to scale the marketing function of your organization. These include:

- Channel and Campaign Performance Report Template (Chapter 1)
- Demand Generation Opportunity versus Effort Mapping Template (Chapter 2)
- Multiproduct Line Content Roadmap Template (Chapter 3)
- Marketing Team Structure Example Deck (Chapter 4)
- Marketing Budget Proposal Template (Chapter 5)

You can get access to all the above resources in the form of spreadsheets and documents at www.howtosaas.com/bookresources.

ACKNOWLEDGMENTS

I'd like to thank the following people, who were essential in my journey to building the frameworks, experiences, and expertise shared in this book:

- Dmitry Buterin, Founder and former CEO of Wild Apricot
- Zane Tarence, Managing Director of Founders Advisors
- Bryce Youngren, Managing Partner at Polaris Partners
- Michael Libert, Senior Vice President at TA Associates
- David Nokes, CEO at Emergency Reporting
- Lacey Ford, former SVP of Marketing at insightsoftware
- Mike Devine, CMO of HelpSystems
- Donald Cowper, Director of Marketing at Wild Apricot
- Farhad Chikhliwala, former Director of Marketing at Wild Apricot
- Our entire team at How To SaaS, with whom this framework was built
- Our clients at How To SaaS, whom we get the pleasure of serving every day
- My wife, Neha, for supporting me and How To SaaS from the beginning
- My daughter, Lyla, for inspiring me to chase my dreams

ABOUT THE AUTHOR

SHIV NARAYANAN is the Founder and CEO of How To SaaS, a management consulting firm that helps private equity firms and their portfolio companies drive enterprise value with marketing. Previously, Shiv was the CMO of Wild Apricot, which was acquired by Rubicon Technology Partners in 2017 and flipped to Pamlico Capital in 2018. Shiv is also an advisor and mentor to technology startups from accelerators like Y Combinator, Techstars, 500 Startups, and the Kellogg-Schulich Executive MBA Program.

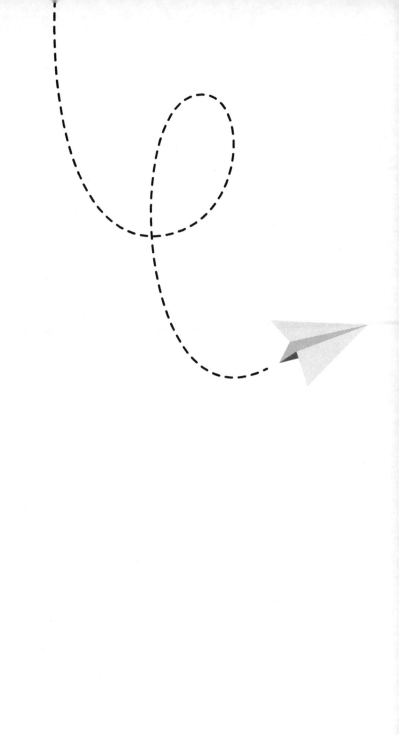

Made in United States
Troutdale, OR
11/27/2024